YOU CAN'T GET RID OF ME THAT EASILY!

By David Farrell

© Copyright 2018 by David Farrell
All rights reserved.
This book or any portion thereof may not be
reproduced or used in any manner whatsoever
without the express written permission of the publisher
except for th use of brief quotations in a book review.

Printed in Australia.
First Printing 2018.

ISBN: 978-1-64467-910-4

FOR JADE & DYLAN

Roger was an apple tree.

Adam was a cheeky apple.

When it was time for the fruit to fall
Adam said 'NO!'
'You can't get rid of me that easily.'

Roger tried to tell Adam that everything would be alright.
Adam shook his head.
'NO! You can't get rid of me that easily!'

Roger gave his branches
a gentle shake...

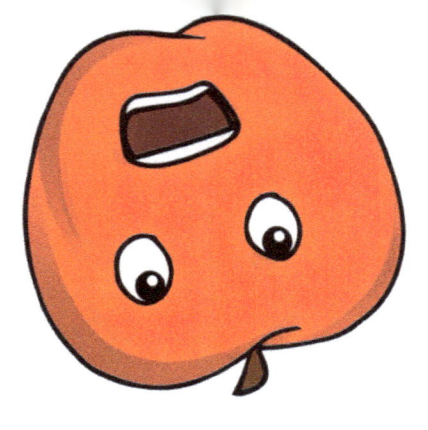

Charlie fell.
Lucy fell.
Oscar fell.
But Adam held on.
'You can't get rid of me that easily!'

Farmer Webster came and picked some apples.

Belinda was picked.
Eve was picked.
Jack was picked.

But Adam hid.

'You can't get rid of me that easily...' he whispered.

Soon Adam was the last apple on the tree.

One day a hungry worm crawled up Roger's trunk.

He spotted Adam
and licked his lips.
'Help save me!' cried Adam.

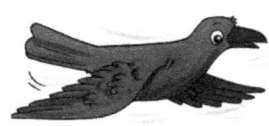

Roger didn't want Adam to get eaten by the worm.

He shook his branches and the worm fell to the ground.

'Ha ha!' laughed Adam.
'I'm staying here forever!'

A black crow heard Adam laughing and flew over to him.

He started to peck Adam!

Adam tried to hold on
but it was no use.
Finally he fell to the ground.

Things weren't the same after that. Roger missed Adam and his cheeky face.

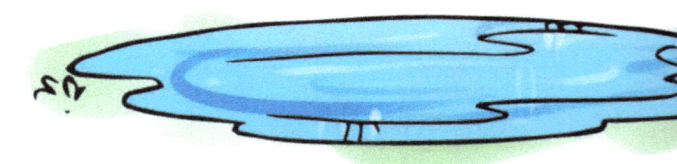

As time went by
something started to grow...

and grow...

and GROW!

'Adam? Is that you?'

'You can't get rid of me that easily!' said Adam with a smile.

www.ingramcontent.com/pod-product-compliance
Lightning Source LLC
Chambersburg PA
CBHW061129070526
44584CB00033B/4269